A World of Difference

# Pass the Bread!

By Karin Luisa Badt

CHILDRENS PRESS®
CHICAGO

## Picture Acknowledgements

Cover (top left), NASA; cover (center left), © The Anthony Blake Photo Library; cover (bottom), © Robert Frerck/Odyssey/Chicago; Cover (top right), SuperStock International, Inc.; 1, © The Anthony Blake Photo Library; 3 (top), © Ducatez/JPDB/Photri; 3 (center), © The Anthony Blake Photo Library; 3 (bottom), © Christine Osborne/Valan; 4 (left), © Buddy Mays/Travel Stock; 4 (right), © Robert Frerck/Odyssey/Chicago; 5 (top left), © John Cancalosi/Valan; 5 (top right), © Chad Ehlers/Tony Stone Images; 5 (bottom), © Robert Frerck/Odyssey/Chicago; 6 (top), © Victor Englebert; 6 (bottom left), © Ken Patterson/Valan; 6 (bottom center), © Robert Frerk/Odyssey/Chicago; 7 (top), © The Anthony Blake Photo Library; 7 (center), © Jerry Koser/H. Armstrong Roberts; 7 (bottom) and 8 (top and center), © Victor Englebert; 8 (bottom) and 9 (top), © Dr. George K. Peck/Ivy Images; 9 (center), © Victor Englebert; 9 (bottom), © Ann Purell; 10 (top and center), The Anthony Blake Photo Library; 10 (bottom), © Leslye Borden/PhotoEdit; 11 (top and bottom), The Anthony Blake Photo Library; 12 (top), © Robert Frerck/Odyssey/Chicago; 12 (center), © Ducatez/JPDB/Photri; 13 (top), © Michael Rutherford/SuperStock International, Inc.; 13 (center), SuperStock International, Inc.; 13 (bottom), © Reinhard Brucker; 14 (top), © Jason Laure'; 14 (bottom), © Tom Brownold/Root Resources; 15 (top), © Victor Englebert; 15 (center), © Reinhard Brucker/Field Museum, Chicago; 15 (bottom) and 16 (top and bottom), © The Anthony Blake Photo Library; 17 (top left), © Mary A. Root/Root Resources; 17 (top right), © Victor Englebert; 17 (bottom left), © Amy Reichman/Envision; 17 (bottom right), © Robert Frerck/Odyssey/Chicago; 18 (top), © Cameramann International, Ltd.; 18 (center), © Reinhard Brucker/Milwaukee Public Museum; 18 (bottom), © Robert Frerck/Odyssey/Chicago; 19 (top left), © Steven Rothfeld/Tony Stone Images; 19 (top right), © John Eastcott/Yva Momatiuk/Valan; 19 (bottom), © Cameramann International, Ltd.; 20 (top), © Buddy Mays/Travel Stock; 20 (center), Photri; 20 (bottom), © Cameramann International, Ltd.; 21 (top and bottom) © Victor Englebert; 22 (top), © Felicia Martinez/PhotoEdit; 22 (bottom left), © Amy C. Etra/PhotoEdit; 22 (bottom right), © Jim Shippee/Unicorn Stock Photos; 23 (top left), © K. Ghani/Valan; 23 (top right), © Hamish Wilson/Panos Pictures; 24 (top), © Alan Oddie/PhotoEdit; 24 (bottom left), © Tony Morrison/South American Pictures; 24 (bottom right), © Reinhard Brucker; 25 (top), © Nowitz/Photri; 25 (center), UPI/Bettmann; 26 (top), © The Anthony Blake Photo Library; 26(bottom), Reuters/Bettmann; 27 (top), © Tony Morrison/South American Pictures; 27 (bottom), © C. Osborne/Valan; 28 © Jean Higgins/Unicorn Stock Photos; 29 (top left), © Florent Flipper/Unicorn Stock Photos; 29 (top right), Reuters/Bettmann; 30 (top), UPI/Bettmann; 30 (bottom), Stock Montage; 31 (top and bottom), Reuters/Bettmann

**On the cover**
Top: Baking-powder biscuits
Middle: Bulgarian Schumen loaf
Bottom: Boy delivering fresh bread from bakery,
    Cappadocia, Turkey

**On the title page**
Middle Eastern pita bread

**Project Editor**  Shari Joffe
**Design**  Herman Adler Design Group
**Photo Research**  Feldman & Associates

Badt, Karin Luisa.
    Pass the bread! / by Karin Luisa Badt.
        p. cm. — (A world of difference)
    Includes index.
    ISBN 0-516-08191-8
    1. Bread — Juvenile literature.   [1. Bread.]   I. Series.
GT2868.B33  1995
394.1`2 — dc20                        94-38003
                                           CIP
                                           AC

# Contents

The Staff of Life . . . . . . . . . . . . . . . . . . . . . . . . . . . 4

Wheat, Rye, or Corn? . . . . . . . . . . . . . . . . . . . . . . . 6

Raised or Flat? . . . . . . . . . . . . . . . . . . . . . . . . . . . 12

Homemade or Store-bought? . . . . . . . . . . . . . . . . . 18

Bread as a Utensil . . . . . . . . . . . . . . . . . . . . . . . . 22

Bread to Celebrate! . . . . . . . . . . . . . . . . . . . . . . . 24

Those Who Lack Bread . . . . . . . . . . . . . . . . . . . . . 28

Breaking Bread . . . . . . . . . . . . . . . . . . . . . . . . . . 30

Glossary . . . . . . . . . . . . . . . . . . . . . . . . . . . . . . . 32

Index . . . . . . . . . . . . . . . . . . . . . . . . . . . . . . . . . 32

# The Staff of Life

Have you ever heard people refer to bread as the "staff of life"? Do you know what they mean by that? A *staff* is a long stick that is held in one hand and used for support when walking. Bread is called the "staff of life" because, for thousands of years, it has supported human life in places throughout the world.

Just what is bread? In its simplest form, bread is a food made from grain that has been ground into flour, mixed with water to form dough, and baked into loaves, rolls, or flat sheets.

Ever since ancient times, people have been thankful for their daily bread. Traditionally, the Chinese believed that rice and other grains were gifts from God. Arabs in the Middle East call bread *eish,* which means "life." And, until recently, it was the custom in parts of eastern Europe to kiss bread that had been dropped on the floor.

Today, bread is a staple— a basic food—in many different parts of the world. But the kind of bread people eat varies from culture to culture. Bread

**Moscow, Russia**

**Lamu, Kenya**

New Mexico, United States

Munich, Germany

can be made from a wide variety of grains and plant substances, and comes in many different shapes, sizes, textures, and flavors. It may be dark or light, hard or soft, chewy or fluffy, spicy or mild, salty or sweet or sour! Let's take a look at the different kinds of bread eaten around the world!

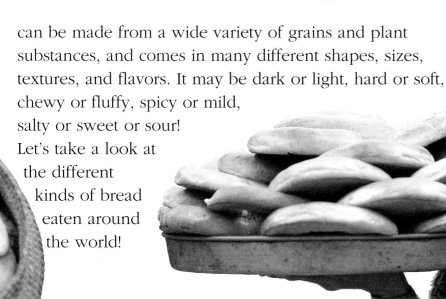

Cappadocia, Turkey

# Wheat, Rye, or Corn?

The primary ingredient in bread is usually grain. Bread can be made from any kind of grain—corn, wheat, oats, millet, barley, rice, or rye. One reason for the variety of breads around the world is that different grains grow well in different environments: millet in dry hot areas of India and Africa; rye in the cold climate of Northern Europe; wheat in North America and the Middle East; barley in the rugged mountains of Tibet and Afghanistan; rice in the Far East.

But bread doesn't have to be made with grain. In some places, bread is made with other kinds of plant substances, such as buckwheat, or even potatoes. In England, up until the 1600s, poor people used to make their bread out of dried peas and beans! In Brazil, thin, flat cakes are made from cassava, a starchy root plant.

**Winnowing barley, Ecuador**
After grain is harvested, it is winnowed to separate the edible seeds from the rest of the plant. Barley bread is common in mountainous countries like Ecuador and Bolivia, because barley grows well at high altitudes.

**People harvesting wheat, India**
A grain is any type of grass that has starchy, edible seeds. Thousands of years ago, people began cultivating wild grasses to make them into crops for food. Different wild grasses were native to different habitats; buckwheat in Russia, corn in the Americas, rye in northern Europe, rice in the wetlands of Asia. Wheat thrives in temperate areas, but can be grown in a wide range of climates and soils. Today, it is the world's most widely grown grain and the most popular grain for making bread.

**Scottish oat bread (center loaf)**
Oats grow well in damp climates, such as those found in Scotland, Switzerland, and Norway.

**Grinding barley, Bolivia**
After the grain is winnowed, it is ground to make flour. The flour can then be used to make bread!

**American corn bread** Corn, or maize, is native to the Americas. Native Americans began planting corn thousands of years ago. North American Indians made porridges and breads out of cornmeal and water, which they cooked on stones over an open fire. In the 1600s, English settlers learned how to make corn bread, which they called "johnnycake," from the Indians. Today, people in the United States still enjoy bread and muffins made from corn.

**Bundles of millet outside clay storage buildings, Niger**

**Selling millet at a local market, Niger** Millet, which can thrive in very hot, dry regions, is commonly used to make bread in desert areas of Africa.

**White bread and whole-grain bread** Whole-grain bread is better for you than white bread. That's because the "whole grain" is used in making the flour. White breads use flour that is made from just the inside of the seed. The husk, the most nutritious part of the grain, has been removed. Despite this, white bread was considered superior to dark whole-grain bread for hundreds of years. One reason was that grain could easily get dirty in the milling process. If the bread was dark, the miller could hide the dirt. White bread would show any specks, so the miller had to be especially careful in making it! However, millers —and bakers—sometimes did terrible things with bread to make it look white. Some ancient Roman bakers, for example, added chalk to their bread!

**Polish rye bread** Rye bread is common in Germany, Russia, Poland, and Scandinavia, because rye is able to survive colder winters than most grains.

**Woman making cassava bread, Brazil** Cassava is a starchy root plant that grows in warm, wet parts of South America. Indians of the Amazon rain forest grind cassava into meal and bake it into flat, hard cakes.

**Chinese rice bread** In most East Asian countries, people prefer rice, eaten as a grain, to bread, but they also may eat breads and dumplings made from rice flour or wheat flour.

People in different places also flavor their breads differently, according to what ingredients are available in their environment. In countries that border the Mediterranean Sea, like Italy, bakers often put salty olives in their bread dough. Olives grow well in the warm, mild climate of the Mediterranean region. In Hungary, bread flavored with poppy seeds is popular. And in Jamaica, a tropical country, many breads are flavored with coconut!

Of course, the kind of bread eaten in a certain country also depends on cultural preferences and customs. In Portugal, for example, people like to eat a traditional fluffy sweet bread called *pao-doce*. In Ireland, soda bread, a traditional chewy bread made with soured milk, is popular.

**Portuguese sweetbread**

**Caribbean banana bread**

**Irish soda breads**

**English saffron bread with raisins** Saffron is a bright yellow herb used to season various foods in Europe and India. Some English, Balkan, and Scandinavian breads are flavored with saffron.

**Italian olive bread**

# Raised or Flat?

Although there are thousands of different kinds of bread around the world, all can be divided into two basic types: raised breads (also called leavened breads) and flat breads.

The earliest breads were flat. About 12,000 years ago, people took grain, smashed it with a stone, and then mixed it with a little water. Then they spread the paste on a stone and cooked it over a fire. The result was flat and hard—like a cracker.

The ancient Egyptians discovered how to make bread rise, or puff up. Around 5,500 years ago, they noticed that when wheat dough was left sitting around, it began to expand. Why? Because of a natural chemical process called fermentation. Tiny fungi called yeasts float around everywhere in the air, waiting to land on something warm, wet, and sweet. When they attach themselves to wheat dough, they give off carbon dioxide gas, which produces air bubbles inside the dough. The Egyptians figured out a way to improve the process by adding more yeast to the dough. When the dough was baked, the bubbles remained trapped inside, producing a light, fluffy loaf instead of a hard, flat one!

**Ancient Egyptians harvesting wheat**
The Egyptians realized that you couldn't make raised bread by cooking it over an open fire, because drafts made the dough go flat. So they invented the first ovens: hollow, cone-shaped containers made of clay. Leavened bread soon became so highly valued that Egyptians used it to pay for things!

**Quick breads** Quick breads—like biscuits, scones, and muffins—are raised breads leavened with baking powder or baking soda instead of yeast. They are called "quick" because you don't have to wait for the dough to rise before you put it in the oven; it rises while it's baking! Quick breads didn't exist until the invention of baking powder in the 1800s. Scones (left) are a sweet quick bread popular in England.

Today, both flat breads and raised breads are eaten throughout the world. Raised breads tend to be most popular in areas where wheat or rye grows plentifully, such as the United States and many European countries. This is because wheat and rye are the only grains that have enough gluten (an elastic protein substance) to react with yeast and produce raised loaves.

To make raised bread from other grains—such as corn—one has to add wheat flour or other leavening agents like baking soda or baking powder.

**American biscuits** Quick breads are especially popular in the United States. Yeast bread was a rare treat for pioneers traveling west in the 1800s. Few brought ovens with them, or had the time to wait for bread to rise and bake. Instead, people made biscuits and pancakes.

**Bohemian Holska bread** This yeast bread, filled with raisins, is eaten in the Czech Republic.

In areas where such grains as millet, oats, buckwheat, barley, or corn are more common—such as parts of the Middle East, Asia, Africa, and Latin America—flat breads are popular. For example, in Central American countries, where corn is a staple crop, people eat thin, flat, corn tortillas. Pueblo Indians in the southwestern part of the United States eat a paper-thin cornbread called *piki,* which is served rolled-up. In Sweden, the traditional bread is a flat bread made of barley. In the Far East, people make a variety of flat breads from rice flour.

**Unleavened corn cake, Nigeria**

**Woman making tortillas, Guatemala** For thousands of years, Indians in Mexico and Central America soaked cornmeal in lime water, formed it into thin, flat cakes, and baked them on pottery griddles called *comales.* When the Spanish came, they adopted this kind of bread and gave it the name by which it is known today: *tortilla.*

**Berber women baking barley flat bread in a village oven, Morocco**
Because it can survive dry heat better than many other grains, Barley is a staple food of people who live in the near-desert areas of North Africa.

**Hopi *piki* bread**

**Swedish *knäckebröd*** Crisp flat breads made with barley are popular in Sweden.

Sometimes, people prefer flat breads, even if they do make them with wheat. Throughout the Middle East, people eat a round, slightly raised wheat bread called *khobz* or *eish*—what English-speaking people call "pita bread." A *khobz* can be sliced open and filled with all sorts of delicious foods, like lamb or hummus, a tasty paste made from chick-peas. In northern India, people eat a variety of whole-wheat flat breads, including crispy *chapati;* soft, spongy *naan;* thin, delicate *pappadam;* and light, puffed-up *puri*.

In some parts of the world, people eat stiff porridges in place of bread. For example, in much of Africa, people eat *fufu,* a sticky dough made out of water and ground-up plant foods like cassava, yam, or plantain. People squeeze the *fufu* into a ball in their right hand and use it to scoop up sauce and meat.

**Middle Eastern pita bread**
In most of the Middle East, people eat pita. However, each country has its own varieties—and exceptions. For example, in Iraq, people may eat *sang-gak,* a slightly raised, spongy bread, while in Jordan, people sometimes prefer round sesame rings known as *ka'ik*.

**Indian *pappadam*** In India, people make several different kinds of flat bread, including a paper-thin fancy bread called *pappadam*.

**Breadfruit** Breadfruit is a starchy tropical fruit that has the color and texture of bread when baked or roasted. It is a staple food in many parts of Polynesia.

**Woman making *popoi,* Marquesas** On some Polynesian islands, people eat *popoi,* a porridge made by beating breadfruit pulp into a paste.

**Grilled *polenta,* Italy** Stiff porridge breads are popular in many parts of the world. In the Friuli region of Italy, for example, the traditional staple is *polenta,* a stiff pudding made of cornmeal and water. In Russia, a porridge called *kasha* is popular. It is made with buckwheat, which grows well in cold, windswept Siberia.

**Woman making *fufu,* Ghana** In Ghana, people eat *fufu* made of plantains (a kind of banana) and yams.

# Homemade or Store-bought?

How do people get their bread? In some countries, including the United States, many people buy their bread already wrapped in plastic at a grocery store. This bread is made in factories, and it may keep fresh for days because of chemicals called preservatives that have been added to it. But in most parts of the world, people buy their bread fresh from small bakeries or street vendors. In Egypt, for example, you would buy bread from a kiosk (a small building with one or more open sides) along the street, where you see hundreds of hot pitas piled up, ready to be eaten. In France, you would buy bread fresh from your local bakery for each meal.

In Iran, you go to a bakery and wait while the baker makes the bread for you. If you are buying a *taftoon* pita, a thin, round bread,

**Buying packaged bread at a grocery store**

**Ancient Roman bakery and bread**

The Romans were the first people after the Egyptians to bake bread in ovens. The Romans also invented the first bakeries, where people could go and buy their bread instead of making it at home. As the influence of the Roman Empire spread, people in other countries began baking bread in ovens as well!

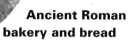

**French bakery** In France, most people buy their bread fresh from a local bakery.

**Inuit family making bread at home, Canada**
Many people throughout the world make their bread at home. This woman is making *bannock* bread, a traditional food of the Inuit people.

you wait while the baker peels it off the oven wall and spokes it out. If, on the other hand, you want a *sangak* pita, a thicker rectangular bread, you wait while the baker scoops it off the stones where it is baked, using a large wooden shovel.

Of course, before there were bakeries, people made their bread at home. Even today, this is still the way most of the world's people get their daily bread.

**Street vendors selling bread, India**

The way people cook bread varies from country to country— and recipe to recipe. Most bread is cooked by being baked in some kind of oven. In the Middle East, for example, people cook their pita in a *tannur*—a cone-shaped clay oven very similar to the kind invented in Egypt over 5,000 years ago. In many European countries, people bake their bread in brick ovens.

**Navajo fry bread**

**Japanese street vendor frying okonomiyaki** *Okonomiyaki* is a type of Japanese pancake that is filled with vegetables and topped with an egg.

**Baking bread in traditional stone ovens:** Germany (left) and Peru (top) Oven-baked breads are generally divided into two types: pan bread, which is baked in a container, and hearth bread, which is baked on a flat pan or directly on the floor of the oven. Both of these pictures show hearth breads. Can you find examples of pan breads in this book?

**Bread baked on an open fire, Ethiopia** These people are baking bread by wrapping dough around stones and surrounding the stones with hot ashes.

Not all bread is baked, however. Navajo Indians, who live in the southwestern United States, fry their bread in a skillet over an open fire. The Inuit people of northern Canada make *bannock,* their traditional bread, in the same way. In Sri Lanka, people cook their breakfast bread—*appa,* a sort of rice pancake—by steaming it in a pan.

# Bread as a Utensil

Bread not only tastes good, it is a highly nutritious food: rich in carbohydrates, vitamins, and minerals. However, there is another reason why bread has been so popular throughout the ages. Bread can be used as an eating utensil! Many people throughout the world use bread as a kind of fork or spoon, to scoop up food. Tortillas in Mexico and Central America, pita bread in the Middle East, and *fufu* in Africa are all used this way. Ethiopians scoop up meat or vegetable stews with pieces of *injera*—a sour, pancakelike bread made of teff flour. Bread can also be used as a kind of plate or bowl. In the Middle Ages, for example, Europeans ate their food on "trenchers" made of stale bread.

**Mexican taco**

**American hot dog** The hot dog is one of the most popular sandwiches in the United States.

**Pita and *baba ganoush*** In Middle Eastern countries, people often use pita to scoop up other foods, such an eggplant dip called *baba ganoush*.

**Chapatis** In Pakistan and India, people often use *chapati* bread to scoop up spicy stews called curries.

**Woman making *injera*, Ethiopia** In Ethiopia, people scoop up spicy stews of meat or vegetables with pieces of *injera,* a sour, spongy, pancakelike bread. *Injera* is made with teff, a grain cultivated in many parts of Africa.

At the end of the meal, they ate the trenchers! In some American restaurants today, you can order chili served in a "bowl" that is actually a hollowed-out loaf of bread, or a salad served in a "bowl" made out of a tortilla. And let's not forget sandwiches! When you eat a sandwich, you need neither a fork nor a plate!

# Bread to Celebrate!

Throughout much of the world, bread is important not only as a food but as a symbol—something that stands for something else. Often, bread is a symbol for food and nourishment. For example, when people in Iran say, "Let's have some bread," they mean, "Let's eat a meal." In English, we say "earn our bread" to mean "earn the necessities of life." We also call the work we do our "bread and butter."

We can see the symbolic importance of bread in many different religious practices. According to the Bible, during the Last Supper before he was crucified, Jesus gave pieces of bread to his disciples and told them that the bread was his body. Today, Christians reenact the Last Supper when they eat a special blessed bread, called the host, as part of the ritual called Communion.

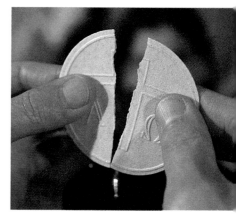

**The Host** The host is the holy bread that symbolizes the body of Christ for Christians. Some Christian faiths use unleavened wafers; others use pieces of leavened bread.

**Bread offerings on All Souls Day, Bolivia** All Souls Day is a Catholic holiday honoring the dead. In many Latin American countries, Catholics visit the graves of their relatives and leave offerings of bread molded into special shapes.

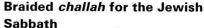

**Braided *challah* for the Jewish Sabbath**

**Matzo at the Passover table**  During the special Passover dinner known as the *Seder,* Jewish people eat a variety of foods that have symbolic meaning, including matzo.

**Swiss man with bread baked for his godchild**  In Switzerland's Loetschen Valley, godparents traditionally present a special loaf of bread at the christening ceremony of their godchildren.

In the Jewish faith, people traditionally eat a braided, egg-rich white bread called *challah* every Friday night to celebrate the Sabbath. On Rosh Hashanah, the Jewish New Year, Jewish people eat a round *challah* to symbolize the cyclical year. And during Passover, Jews eat matzo, a flat, unleavened bread. By eating matzo, they commemorate the time thousands of years ago when their ancestors had to escape from Egypt and did not have time to wait for the bread to rise.

**Greek Easter bread** Special breads made for the Christian holiday of Easter often have eggs baked in them, to symbolize the resurrection of Jesus. In Greece, the Easter bread is called *hsoureki*. It includes raisins and dyed eggs. In Naples, Italy, the special Easter bread is called *casatiello*. It is a cheese bread with salami, peppers, and baked eggs in the middle. In Russia, the traditional Easter bread is *kulich*, made with almonds, raisins, and sugar.

Special breads are an important part of many religious holidays. In Turkey, people eat a special pita called *pide* during Ramadan, the month in which Muslims fast from sunrise to sunset. *Pide* is bigger and chewier than the pita eaten during the other months of the year. Many Christians in Europe eat special breads at Christmastime: Italian *panettone*, German *stollen*, English sugarplum bread, Danish *Julekage*, Greek *Christopsomo*. Most of these breads are sweet and filled with candied fruits and nuts. Sugar, candied fruit, and nuts were—and still are— expensive items. For that reason, they traditionally have been used only on special occasions.

**Priest of the Coptic Orthodox Church blessing loaves of bread during a religious mass, Egypt**

**Peruvians presenting bread to God during Lent**  In many cultures, people offer bread to their god in thanks for their well-being. Lent is a forty-day period of penitence observed by Christians.

***Nahash* for Ramadan**  During Ramadan, the ninth month of the Islamic year, Muslims may not eat or drink from dawn to sunset. At the end of Ramadan, they celebrate with a feast that includes many special foods, including a sweet pastry called *nahash*.

In many cultures around the world, bread is a symbol of prosperity. That is why it is common for people to offer bread to their god in thanks for their well-being. The Zinacantecos Indians in Mexico, for example, offer tortillas to their ancestral gods, whom they believe live in the mountains.

# Those Who Lack Bread

Unfortunately, not everyone in the world has enough bread. More than one billion people—one in every five—do not get as much food as they need. In fact, in some countries, like Zambia, Bhutan, and Bolivia, more than half the children are undernourished.

Food shortages have many different causes. Droughts (periods of little or no rain), floods, and other natural disasters can destroy crops. But often, food shortages are caused by things people do. Deforestation (clearing of forests), overgrazing (allowing cattle and other animals to eat all of the plant life in a place), and erosion (wearing away) of soil due to faulty farm practices—all of these help make land unfit for growing crops. Wars can make it impossible to farm or transport food. Overpopulation is another cause of food shortages. Right now, there are more than five billion people in the world: double the number of people who were alive only fifty years ago! In some countries, there are more people than there is food to eat.

On the average, people get half their calories from grain, making it the world's most important source of food. Grain shortages, such as those that have occurred in Somalia, Sudan, and Haiti, can lead to famine (widespread starvation) and political and social unrest.

Famines were common in Europe during the Middle Ages. In those times, many poor people ate bread for breakfast, lunch, and dinner, so it was extremely important to them. In times of grain shortages, poor people had to

**Bread line in Russia**
In countries where there are massive food shortages, people often have to wait in long lines to get bread.

**Food distribution camp for Kurdish refugees** Refugees are people who flee their country to escape persecution or war. It is often very difficult for refugees to find food and shelter. The Kurds are an ethnic group whose traditional homeland spreads over parts of Turkey, Iraq, and Iran. In the late 1980s, the Iraqi government forced thousands of Kurds to flee from Iraq into Turkey and Iran. Refugee camps were set up near the borders to help provide food and shelter for these Kurds.

make their bread out of acorns and pine bark, with pig's blood added for nourishment.

Throughout history, there have been bread riots in which hungry people have demanded grain from their government. One of the most famous bread riots took place in the 1700s in France. It helped bring about the French Revolution!

**Afghan children** In this 1990 photograph, children hug loaves of bread obtained from government bakeries. People in the northern provinces of Afghanistan were starving following eleven years of war.

# Breaking Bread

reaking bread is an expression that means sharing a meal—and enjoying the company of another person. In fact, the word *companion* is a combination of the Latin words for "together" and "bread." In many cultures, sharing "bread" (food) is an important way of welcoming strangers or of maintaining friendships and family ties.

People also share their bread in another sense. In the United States, for example, you can find Middle Eastern pita, eastern European bagels, Ethiopian *injera,* Mexican *tortillas,* Italian pizza, and countless other breads from countries all over the world. These once-foreign breads are a part of many Americans' daily diets.

Bread has traveled around the world mostly because of explorers, colonizers, and immigrants who brought their native culture—and breads—to new places. In Japan, people occasionally eat *kasatera*. This is a yellow sponge bread brought by Spanish traders to Japan in the 1500s. In Morocco, the French *baguette* is a popular bread. France ruled Morocco in the first half of the 1900s.

**"American" bakery in Turkey**

**American Indians teaching Europeans how to grow corn, 1600s**

The grains from which bread is made also have traveled from place to place. Corn, for example, was unknown to Europeans before Columbus came to the Americas. European explorers brought corn back home, and eventually this yellow grain became a staple around the world! America also benefited from the arrival of the Europeans, who brought wheat with them. Until then, wheat had never grown in America; its native grains are corn, wild rice, quinoa, and amaranth. Today, the United States produces and exports half of the wheat in the world.

**Women welcoming Russian leader Boris Yeltsin to Urdmurtia**  It is a custom in many parts of the world to welcome visitors by offering them bread.

In Kenya, Indian bread is popular, because many Indians moved to Kenya to escape famines in India. In Iran, a popular bread is *barbari,* a thick, crusty, chewy pita. *Barbari* was originally a Turkish bread. Turkish immigrants brought this kind of bread with them when they came to live in Iran. What kind of bread do you usually eat? Do you know where it originated?

**French bread in Vietnam**  The French bread still sold today in Vietnam is a reminder that Vietnam was once a French colony.

# Glossary

**ancestral** having to do with relatives who lived in the past (p.27)

**ancient** very old (p.4)

**carbohydrates** energy-rich nutrients composed of carbon, hydrogen, and oxygen (p.22)

**climate** the average weather conditions of a region over a period of years (p.7)

**colonizer** one who comes to a foreign place to found a settlement governed by a distant country (p.30)

**commemorate** to recall to mind (p.25)

**cultivate** to raise or assist the growth of crops by tilling or by labor and care (p.6)

**culture** the beliefs and customs of a group of people that are passed from one generation to another (p.4)

**custom** the usual way of doing things (p.4)

**cyclical** referring to a series of events that always happens in the same order (p.25)

**environment** a person's natural surroundings (p.6)

**ethnic group** a group of people whose members share the same culture, language, or customs (p.29)

**harvest** to gather and bring in a crop (p.6)

**hearth** the floor of a fireplace, furnace, or oven (p.21)

**leavened** raised (p.12)

**necessities** the things we need (p.24)

**nourishment** food (p.24)

**offering** a sacrifice offered as part of worship (p.24)

**originate** to bring or come into existence (p.31)

**penitence** sincere sorrow for one's sins or wrongful acts (p.27)

**persecution** mistreatment or oppression because of religion, race, or beliefs (p.29)

**porridge** a soft food made by boiling grain in water or milk until it thickens (p.7)

**preference** a choosing or special liking of one thing over another (p.10)

**preservatives** a substance added to food to prevent it from spoiling (p.18)

**resurrection** a rising from the dead (p.26)

**traditional** handed down from generation to generation (p.4)

**trencher** a platter for serving food (p.22)

**undernourished** not getting enough food to stay healthy or grow (p.28)

**vitamins** a group of organic substances found in most natural foodstuffs and required for proper health (p.22)

**wafer** a thin crisp cake or cracker (p.24)

**winnow** to sift; sort out (p.6)

# Index

Afghanistan, 6, 29
Africa, 6, 14, 16, 22, 23
bakeries, 18, 19
barley, 6, 7, 14, 15
Bhutan, 28
Bolivia, 7, 24, 28
Brazil, 6, 9
buckwheat, 6, 14
Canada, 19, 21
cassava, 6, 9, 16
China, 4, 9
corn, 6, 7, 14, 30
Czech Republic, 13
Ecuador, 6
Egypt, 12, 18, 20, 26
England, 6, 11, 13
Ethiopia, 21, 22, 23, 30
Europe, 4, 6, 11, 22, 26, 30
Far East, 6, 9, 14
flat breads, 12-17
flavorings, 10-11
flour, 4, 7, 8
food shortages, 28-29
France, 18, 19, 30
Germany, 5, 9, 21
Ghana, 17
grains, 4, 5, 6, 12, 14, 28
Greece, 26
Guatemala, 14
Haiti, 28
Hungary, 10
India, 6, 11, 16, 19, 23, 31
Iran, 18, 29, 31
Iraq, 16, 29
Ireland, 10, 11
Italy, 10, 17, 30
Jamaica, 10
Japan, 20. 30
Jordan, 16

Kenya, 4, 31
Latin America, 14
Mexico, 14, 22, 27, 30
Middle East, 4, 6, 14, 16, 20, 22, 30
millet, 6, 8, 14
Morocco, 15, 30
Niger, 8
Nigeria, 14
Norway, 7
oats, 6, 7, 14
ovens, 12, 18, 20, 21
Pakistan, 23
Peru, 21, 27
Poland, 9
Polynesia, 17
Portugal, 10
quick breads, 13
raised breads, 12-17
religion, 24-26
rice, 4, 6, 9, 14, 21
Romans, 18
Russia, 4, 9, 17, 28, 31
rye, 6, 9
Scandinavia, 9, 11
Scotland, 7
Somalia, 28
Sri Lanka, 21
Sudan, 28
Sweden, 14, 15
Switzerland, 7, 25
Tibet, 6
Turkey, 5, 26, 29, 31
United States, 5, 7, 13, 14, 18, 21, 22, 30
Vietnam, 31
wheat, 6, 12, 16, 30
Zambia, 28

# About the Author

**Karin Luisa Badt** has a Ph.D. in comparative literature from the University of Chicago and a B.A. in literature and society from Brown University. She likes to travel and live in foreign countries. Ms. Badt has taught at the University of Rome and the University of Chicago.